RISC-V
an Open Source Solution for Space Flight Computers

Patrick H. Stakem

(c) 2018, 2022

Table of Contents

Introduction

Pronounced RISK-Five, RISC-V is the latest implementation of the MIPS architecture, in an open source configuration. The project kicked off in 2010 at the University of California, Berkeley.

It had been announced in 2018. Multiple companies now offer RISC-V chips, and the architecture is compatible with several FPGA's. The RISC-V architecture is making inroads on the popular ARM embedded architecture.

There have been numerous space missions using the MIPS architecture. One of these, New Horizons, is currently sending back data from outside our solar system. The big problem is radiation damage to electronics. RISC-V has a solution to this.

It is hard to generalize about the RISC approach, because for every principle discussed, a counter-example in implementation can be found. However, in RISC, most instructions execute in one cycle. RISC machines tend to have a small instruction set, and complex instructions are built up from primitive ones. This follows the observation that, generally, the simple instructions are the most frequently used and the more complex instructions less so. The use of the RISC technique began around 1990, and has now become mainstream. It evolved out of a time when memory was an expensive asset, and memory utilization was an issue.

Decoding instructions and addressing modes are a major bottleneck to speed, so simplified instruction encoding and limited data addressing modes are preferable.

Single cycle execution improves interrupt latency and response determinism. A load/store architecture will have many on-chip registers to hold data currently in use. A RISC CPU is tightly coupled to memory, and achieves a high data bandwidth with a sophisticated cache. Instruction execution is pipelined. Instruction decoding is streamlined because there are fewer instructions, and they are relatively simple, with perhaps only a single address mode. In a RISC machine, microcode is avoided, yet some RISC architectures use it.

Here's a top level approach to a RISC implementation. Eliminate all instructions that can't execute in 1 clock cycle. Move complexity from hardware to software. Add more hardware, as feasible, to include more complex instructions. There are no subroutines or loops at the machine language level allowed. Don't slow down the majority of instructions in favor of the minority.

The 90/10 rule says that about 90% of real code are simple instructions, such as load/store, ALU ops, etc. Not much can be done to speed up the remaining 10% of complex instructions.

The instructions/task metric is low for CISC; high for RISC; i.e., RISC uses more instructions to get the job done, but they are faster instructions. Non-RISC instructions get more done, per instruction.

There's a lot of material on RISC-V on the Internet. The MIPS architecture has flown on numerous spacecraft, facing the challenging problems of radiation damage. Now that we have an open source ISA, we can consider the architecture of a RISC-V implemented on a Rad-Hard FPGA.

RISC-V architectures have been implemented in India, China, and other countries around the globe.

Author

The author received his BSEE from Carnegie Mellon University, and Masters in Computer Science and Applied Physics from the Johns Hopkins University. He has always worked in the aerospace sector, supporting NASA projects at all of the NASA Centers. He has taught for the graduate Engineering Science and Computer Science Departments at Loyola University in Maryland, andEmbedded Systems for the Johns Hopkins University, Whiting School of Engineering, He developed and taught a course in RISC architecture for Loyola College (now, University) in Maryland He participated in several of NASA/GSFC's Summer Engineering Boot Camp Programs, leading international teams of students on projects.

The author can be found on Facebook and Linkedin.

MIPS Architecture

Meaning "microprocessor without interlocking stages," the MIPS architecture was the brainchild of John Hennessy at Stanford University. It was produced by multiple manufacturers, and initially addressed the workstation market. MIPS, the company, was the first to ship a commercial RISC processor, in 1985. The company was eventually bought by SGI. MIPS was the keeper of the architectural specification (IP) of the chips, with various company's producing variants under license.

There were several architectural models of the MIPS chip. The R-2000 was a 32-bit load/store machine with associated MMU and floating point chips. There were 32 registers, with R0=0, and R31 held the link address for a branch. The R-3000 was also 32-bit, and was produced in various versions for the embedded market. The R-4000 was a 64-bit machine with integral co-processors.

The R-2000 chip was an integer CPU with a 5-stage pipeline, and 32 32-bit registers. All instructions were a standard 32-bits in length for ease of decode and pipelining. The architecture allowed for 1 to 4 co-processors, tightly coupled. CR0 was defined as the system control processor, the MMU. CR1 was the floating point processor. The five-stage pipeline included stations for fetch, decode, ALU, memory access, and write. The compiler was responsible for inserting a NOP instruction after any instruction using the results of a previous instruction. This is the "no interlocking stages" part.

The 1988 R-3000 processor was a Harvard architecture internally, having separate data and instruction paths. It supported multiprocessing. There was an associated R-3010 floating point co-processor. The floating point unit had its own set of 32 x 32-bit registers, and used a 6-stage pipeline. The R3000 had an integral 64-entry translation look-aside buffer. Many embedded variations of the R-3000 architecture were produced.

The 1994 R-4000 was a true 64-bit chip, with 64-bit address bus, registers, ALU, and data paths. It was a dual-issue, 8-stage pipeline design. The later R-6000 was implemented in very fast yet power-hungry ECL technology.

The MIPS architecture was bi-endian, supporting both little-endian or big-endian mode, select-able at reset.

MMX extensions

In addition, the latest versions of MIPS have MMX extensions for video and graphics processing, and SSE extensions for SIMD. The MDMX, MIPS' Digital Media Extensions, address 3-D graphics transforms. These are, at the moment, integer only.

MMX is a single-instruction multiple-data (SIMD) extension to the architecture. It includes 64-bit registers. These registers are meant to hold eight 8-bit integers, four 16-bit integers, or two 32-bit integers, which will be operated upon in parallel.

MMX supports saturation arithmetic. In this scheme, all operations are limited to a fixed range between a defined minimum and maximum. Values beyond those limits are not recognized. The mathematical properties of associativity and distributivity are not applicable in saturation arithmetic. An alternative to saturation arithmetic is where the values wrap-around, which unfortunately changes the sign in two's-complement representation. For audio processing (louder-than-loud) and video processing (blacker-than-black), saturation arithmetic works fine. It's the issue of getting an answer "close enough" in the time allowed. Saturation arithmetic plays an important role in digital signal processing techniques for video and audio processing.

In 1999, Intel introduced the Streaming SIMD Extensions (SSE) architecture. This has new 128-bit registers, and a corresponding instruction set extension. An SSE and a floating point instruction cannot be issued in the same cycle, due to on-chip resource conflicts. SSE2 introduced double precision floating point support. SSE has 70 additional instructions to support operations for digital signal processing and graphics. SSE3 added new digital signal processing features, and SSE4 added an instruction for vector dot product. This was adopted by many chip manufacturers.

Advanced Vector Extensions (AVX) introduced a 256-bit data path, and 3-operand instructions. These units can operate on 256 or 512 bit data structures. AVX-2 extends integers to 256 bits, and adds bit manipulation and multiply. AVX-512 extends data and operations to 512 bits. Vector data can be loaded from non-contiguous memory locations, referred to as "gather", and stored to non-contiguous locations, called scatter. Exponential and reciprocal instructions accelerate transcendental functions. They implement the fused multiply-add operation, which looks like: $X = round (a \times b + c)$. MIPS-3D has new functions to handle 3D graphics.

Virtualization

We should take a moment and look at virtualization, and the included hardware support. MIPS virtualization allows for multiple operating systems to share base resources simultaneously, and is an example of hardware supported virtualization.

A computer is a general-purpose machine with compute, memory and input/output resources. We can virtualize any or all of these resources.

Virtualization is an isomorphism from guest to host, if we want to get mathematical. We map the guest state to the host state, implement equivalent functions, and we get one machine pretending to be another, or a bunch of "others." The key is, if you can touch it, it is the physical machine, the host. Otherwise it is the guest. Just like a guest at a resort, you get access to the resources you've paid for, but not total access. That's reserved for management.

There are many ways to do this. We can have hardware

virtualization, where the host machine acts like a real machine with a real operating system that is stand-alone. Most importantly, it can act like several real machines.

We can have full virtualization, which is a complete or nearly complete simulation of the existing hardware. This allows the guest operating system and its applications to run unmodified.

We can also have partial virtualization, where some but not all of the host are available. The guest operating system and the applications may need to be modified.

In para-virtualization, the hardware environment is not simulated, but the guests operating systems need to be aware of the hypervisor. They are slightly modified versions of the base operating system. Paravirtualized guests generally run faster because of the lack of the emulation layer.

Virtualization is complex, not just to implement but also to run. If it can get specific assistance from the platform hardware, it can run faster. This is the trend from the chip manufacturers; to add specific virtualization assistance in the chip design.

Although virtualization was slow to be adopted in the embedded space, it is now seeing more use, as the chips have enough resources to support it. The MIPS architecture includes virtualization support in hardware. This allows for different application domains, isolated from each other. This is supported in MIPS32 and MIPS64. There is also a compressed instruction set called microMips, consisting of a subset of the main architecture. An emerging variant is "containers."

Embedded

Embedded refers to special purpose computers that are a part of a larger system, as opposed to generic desktop computers, tablets, and servers. Embedded systems are for specific purposes; they are not necessarily general purpose. They may have a limited or no human interface, but usually support complex I/O. The embedded computer can be characterized by the parameters of its central processing unit, memory, and input/output (I/O). The CPU parameters of importance are speed, power consumption, and price. The memory parameters include power consumption, speed, volatility, and size or capacity. I/O characteristics must be matched to external systems components, and there are many options.

Most microprocessors sold, by volume, are destined for embedded applications. They are purpose-built, and self-contained. Many include the features of BIST – built-in self-test. Most of the embedded market is currently dominated by the ARM architecture.

Although not a requirement, embedded computer systems are usually constructed from monolithic microprocessor chips. Previous generations have involved minicomputers. The air traffic control system is a large dedicated embedded system based on mainframes. Modern embedded systems might be hosted on Field Programmable Gate Arrays (FPGA), or use a custom Application Specific Integrated Circuit (ASIC).

System, as I use the word here, refers to the computer, memory, input-output, and the associated devices that the embedded computer controls or communicates with.

The Flight Computer market for spacecraft is a special purpose, low volume market, extremely niche. This is mostly due to the operating environment.

MIPS Embedded

Competent in high performance computing, MIPS also has implementations in the embedded space. The architecture is called MIPS-32 and MIPS-64. There are multiple chip manufactures producing silicon based on these definitions. Various company implemented embedded versions of the MIPS architecture, based on the R4000 version. Popular in spaceflight, the MIPS-based Mongoose architecture is derived from the LR-3000.

The MIPS-III architecture, first instantiated in the R4000, was implemented by several companies.

MIPS-32

These chips support virtualization and SIMD. Up to 4 megabytes of instruction and data cache was supported as well

MIPS-64

MIPS-64 is an extension to the MIPS-32 architecture. It features high performance caches. It supports data stream, conditional move, data prefetch, and other advance techniques to enhance throughput performance.

It has 64-bit floating point registers, and supports SIMD. MIPS-64 can host Linux, Android, Windows-CE, and several real-time operating systems.

Open Source versus Proprietary

This is a topic we need to discuss before we get very far into software. It is not a technical topic, but concerns your right to use (and/or own, modify) software. It's those software licenses you click to agree with, and never read. That's what the intellectual property lawyers are betting on.

Software and software tools are available in proprietary and open source versions. Open source software is free and widely available, and may be incorporated into your system. It is available under license, which generally says that you can use it, but derivative products must be made available under the same license. This presents a problem if it is mixed with purchased, licensed commercial software, or a level of exclusivity is required. Major government agencies such as the Department of Defense and NASA have policies related to the use of Open Source software.

14

Adapting a commercial or open source operating system to a particular problem domain can be tricky. Usually, the commercial operating systems need to be used "as-is" and the source code is not available. The software can usually be configured between well-defined limits, but there will be no visibility of the internal workings. For the open source situation, there will be a multitude of source code modules and libraries that can be configured and customized, but the process is complex. The user can also write new modules in this case.

The Open Source Initiative (www.opensource.org) maintains the definition of Open Source, and certifies licenses.

The GNU General Public License (GPL) is the most widely used free software license. It guarantees end users the freedoms to use, study, share, copy, and modify the software. Software that ensures that these rights are retained is called free software. The license was originally written by Richard Stallman of the Free Software Foundation (FSF) for the GNU project in 1989. The GPL is a *copyleft* license, which means that derived works can only be distributed under the same license terms. This is in distinction to permissive free software licenses, of which the BSD licenses are the standard examples. Copyleft is in counterpoint to traditional copyright. Proprietary software "poisons" free software, and cannot be included or integrated with it, without abandoned the GPL. The GPL covers the GNU/linux operating systems and most of the GNU/linux-based applications.

A Vendor's software tools and operating system or application code is usually proprietary intellectual property. It is unusual to get the source code to examine, at least without binding legal documents and additional funds. Along with this, you do get the vendor support. An alternative is open source code, which is in the public domain. There are a series of licenses covering open source code usage, including the Creative Commons License, the gnu public license, copyleft, and others. Open Source describes a collaborative environment for development and testing. Use of open source code carries with it an implied responsibility to "pay back" to the community. Open Source is not necessarily free.

The Open source philosophy is sometimes at odds with the rigidized procedures evolved to ensure software performance and reliability. Offsetting this is the increased visibility into the internals of the software packages, and control over the entire software package. Besides application code, operating systems such as GNU/linux and bsd can be open source. The programming language Python is open source. The popular web server Apache is also open source, as is the database Rbase.

Hardware can be open source as well, or protected by patent.

MIPS Open Initiative

The MIPS Open Initiative was kicked off by Wave Computing in December of 2018. It made an Open Source version of the MIPS 32 and MIPS 64 architectures freely available. It's focus is on the use of MIPS in AI applications, using system-on-a-chip (SoC) approaches. They are also providing MIPS SIMD extensions, DSP extensions, multi-threading support, virtualization, and a memory controller. They also have a microMIPS architecture.

RISC-V

RISC-V is an open source instruction set architecture originating from U. C. Berkeley and based on the MIPS architecture, also from Berkeley. The implementation can be in FPGA format, with the RISC-V Cores or SoC's downloaded from GITHUB. There is a compliance suite that the core SOC has to demonstrate before it can be label RISC-V. This is developed and maintained by the RISC-V Foundation, which currently has more than 100 members. The draft specification is also maintained on GitHub. At this writing there are some 16 instantiations of the RISC-V architecture, with at least that number in development.

In addition to the basic ISA, you can add custom features to your implementation. You can make a system on a chip, with dedicated I/O, and you could do multi-core. The RISC-V foundation says, "using an open-source ISA offers greater flexibility, but it does not include any processor designs. It is up to the licensee to develop a custom processor or license one from another IP vendor, such as SiFive, which would then include some form or license and/or royalty fees to the IP vendor.

A series of open source software tools has been developed for the architecture. This is called the RISC-V Software Ecosystem, and includes the legacy tools for the MIPS processor.

These include C compilers, including GCC, debugging tools, boot loaders, kernels and operating systems, multiple simulators, debugging tools, the Forth kernel, and the GNU Eclipse IDE's. Kernels include linux, RTEMS, and others. Operating systems include Fedora, Debian, openSUSE, open Embedded, FreeBSD, NetBSD, etc.

You can fabricate your own RISC-V, or you can buy a commercial chip. There are currently 5 hardware vendors, with more coming along. The manuals for these devices are available on the RISC-V website.

The RISC-V implementation can also be made Arduino compatible. For example, the Crowd Supply HiFive1 part, running a 320 MHz clock. The chip has 16k of L1 cache, 16k of data sram, and included debugging support. There are a wide variety of I/O devices available, such as UART's, QSPI, PWM, and timers. This approach was used by Intel in it's Arduino-101 design, which was x86-

based. What this approach provides is a Arduino-compatible processor, using a vast ecosystem of hardware, software, and hands-on expertise. The difference is, the "Arduino" is now a 32-bit (or 64-bit) MIPS architecture. You don't need to consider that when you implement a system. Just program it in c using the Arduino libraries. The HiFive1 product from CrowdSupply is an Arduino-compatible board, using a RISC-V architecture, The FE310 chip it uses, from SiFive, is a system-on-a-chip, very basic, and does not address external memory.

The specs on the board are impressive. The E310 cpu is 32-bit, and can run at 320 MHz. There is a 16k I-cache, a 16k data sram, and an associated debug module. On-chip peripherals include UART's, PWM's, and timers. I can be powered from a USB port. There are 19 digital I/O lines and an SPI interface. It can address up to 128 megs of external flash. There is also a 64-bit version, that requires a larger capacity logic device. Including a floating point unit or graphics processing requires even more capacity. If we want to push the edge of the envelope, we can consider multi-processor or multicore architecture on one chip.

What you get when you download a RISC-V IP you get a library of instruction set architecture. You can then program that into an FPGA. The instruction set download is free. The FPGA is not. In the end, the capability you get is less expensive than other methods.

RISC-V implementations in FPGA's

There have been multiple implementations of the RISC-V so far, and more are coming.

HiFive-1

The Arduino HiFive-1 is a RISC-V board from Arduino.org. It was announced just before the Maker Faire Bay Area - 2017. It implements the RISC-V 32-bit architecture in a SiFive E310 SoC. It runs at 320 MHz, with an embedded wifi and bluetooth capability. So, what we have is a 32-bit Arduino architecture presented to the user, while inside, all that runs on a RISC-V MIPS architecture. The Arduino user does not need to be aware of the guts – not an Arm but a MIPS architecture. In building and running code, it is an "Arduino," albeit on steroids.

You can buy this as a hardware board. At vendor Sparkfun, it is currently listed at under $68. It can support a JTAG connection via usb. It has 128 Mb of flash memory, and a boot loader in OTP memory. It can be powered from the usb connection, or a 7-12 volt external supply. It supports Arduino shields, and uses SPI, a UART connection, and standard digital 32 GPIO's at 3.3 or 5 volts. The board supports SPI, PWM, I2C, and interrupts. It comes with a SDK.

It can be programmed in C, or RISC-V assembly, using GCC toolchains. The loader/debugger is located in flash.

The interesting thing is, you can instantiate the RISC-V architecture in a rad-hard FPGA, and you have a space computer.

HiFive Unleashed

This board uses the Freedom U540 Core, a 5-core MIPS architecture. It is implemented on the U540 SoC. It has 8 Gbytes of memory with ECC, and a gigabit ethernet port. There is 32 Mbytes of flash, and it accepts a MicroSD card for non-volatile storage. It is instantiated in a 28 nm process SOC. The board supports JTAG, and has a boot rom.

There are four of the U54 cores, and a single E51 core, all 64 bits, connected by their TileLink fabric. External memory in DDR3 or DDR4 is supported. The E51 core supports hardware performance monitoring as part of the privileged architecture. The E54 cores all include floating point and virtual memory.

For I/O it supports ChipLink, QSPI, I2C, PWM, and has two UARTs. and 16 GPIO's. There are 53 global, and 7 priority interrupts.

Each U54 core has its own private L1 instruction and data caches, which are 8-way set associative, and 32k in size. The E51 core has a 2-way set-associative, 16k instruction cache.

Mode select pins allow for booting from one of several sources. The zeroth stage boot loader looks to a on-chip rom. The first stage boot loader uses the DDR memory. The Berkeley Boot Loader has emulation for soft instructions, and "the User Payload" is used to get to Linux. You can boot from a MicroSD card. The reset vector is located at 1004H. DMA is supported on the various cores.

As of this writing, the HiFive Unleased board is available for $999. but it looks like it is being discontinued.

Rad-Hard MIPS architecture and their Space Missions

Once we leave the vicinity of our home planet, conditions deteriorate quickly. The major issue is radiation, since we are outside of safety of the trapped radiation belts, which provide some protection. This is the major challenge, but there are many known ways to mitigate this problem. Then, there is the thermal problem. We're going somewhere that's hotter (sun-ward), or colder. A big issue is the mission duration. It takes years to get to some of the outer planets, and even if the system is powered off, there can be events that will cause it not to wake up. Missions outside the rather friendly environment of near-Earth face additional challenges that must be addressed.

This section discusses the implementations for MIPS architectures in rad-hard technologies for spaceflight, and describes the missions and results.

What does a spacecraft computer do?

Besides attitude determination and control, the onboard embedded system has a variety of housekeeping tasks to attend to.

Generally, there is a dedicated unit, sometimes referred to as the Command & Data Handler (C&DH) with interfaces with the spacecraft transmitters and receivers, the onboard data storage system, and the flight computer. The C&DH, itself a computer, is in charge of uplinked data (generally, commands), onboard data storage, and data transmission. The C&DH can send received commands directly to various spacecraft components, or can hold them for later execution at a specified time. The C&DH has a direct connection with the science instrument(s) for that data stream. If the science instrument package has many units, there may be a separate science C&DH (SC&DH) that consolidates the sensed data, and hands it over to the C&DH for transmission to the ground. It is also common for the C&DH to hand over all commands related to science instruments to the IC&DH.

Consumables inventory

The spacecraft computer calculates and maintains a table of consumables data, both value and usage rate. This includes available state-of-charge in the batteries, amount of thruster propellant, and any other renewable or consumable asset. This is periodically telemetered to the ground.

Thermal management

The spacecraft electronics needs to be kept within a certain temperature for proper operation. Generally, the only heat source is the Sun, and the only heat sink is deep space. There are options as to how the spacecraft can be oriented. In close orbit to a planet, the planet may also represent a heat source. Automatic thermal louvers can be used to regulate the spacecraft internal temperature. The flight computer's job is to keep the science instrument or communications antennae pointed in the right direction. This might have to be overridden in case the spacecraft is getting too hot or too cold.

Electrical Power/energy management

The flight Computer needs to know the state-of-charge (SOC) of the batteries at all times, and whether current is flowing into or out of the batteries. It the SOC is getting too low, some operations must be suspended, so the solar panels or spacecraft itself can be re-oriented to maximize charging. In some cases, redundant equipment may be turned off, according to a predetermined load-shedding algorithm. If the spacecraft batteries are fully discharged, it is generally the end of the mission, because pointing to the Sun cannot be achieved, except by lucky accident. Spacecraft going beyond Jupiter still rely on RTG's – radioisotope thermoelectric generators.

Antenna Pointing

The spacecraft communications antennae must be pointed to the large antennae on the ground (Earth) or to a communications relay satellite in a higher orbit (for Earth or Mars). The Antennae can usually be steered in two axis, independently of the spacecraft body. This can be accomplished in the Main flight computer, or be a task for the C&DH.

Safe Hold mode

As a last resort, the spacecraft has a safe-hold or survival mode that operates without computer intervention. This usually seeks to orient the spacecraft with its solar panels to the Sun to maximize power, turn off all non-essential systems, and call for help. This can be implemented in a dedicated digital unit. It used to be the case that the safe-hold mode was implemented in analog circuitry.

Science Data Processing

I have not mentioned the science payload. Generally, the science instrument(s) have their own dedicated computers that collect the data and hand it over to the spacecraft Command & Data handling unit to be downlinked with the "housekeeping" data. Some level of science data processing can also be done onboard. As missions go further out, and collect more and more data, there is a need for some processing of the data onboard, which may take years (New Horizons is an example) to get back to Earth.

Here is a definition of the levels of science data processing NASA does. This can ll be done on the ground, on transmitted "raw" data, or the lower levels can be done with a capable onboard computer, such as a RISC-V.

NASA Data Processing Levels Definition

0   Reconstructed, unprocessed instrument and payload data at full resolution, with any and all communications artifacts (e. g., synchronization frames, communications headers, duplicate data) removed.

1a   Reconstructed, unprocessed instrument data at full resolution, time-referenced, and annotated with ancillary information, including radiometric and geometric calibration coefficients and geo-referencing parameters (e. g., platform ephemeris) computed and appended but not applied to the Level 0 data (or if applied, in a manner that level 0 is fully recoverable from level 1a data).

1b   Level 1a data that have been processed to sensor units (e. g., radar backscatter cross section, brightness temperature, etc.); not all instruments have Level 1b data; level 0 data is not recoverable from level 1b data.

2   Derived geophysical variables (e. g., ocean wave height, soil moisture, ice concentration) at the same resolution and location as Level 1 source data.

3   Variables mapped on uniform spacetime grid scales, usually with some completeness and consistency (e. g., missing points interpolated, complete regions mosaicked together from multiple orbits, etc.).

4   Model output or results from analyses of lower level data (i. e., variables that were not measured by the

instruments but instead are derived from these measurements).

Radiation Effects

Modern electronics using semiconductor technology does not like energetic particle hits. It's upsetting, and can lead to permanent damage to the device. But, if we're going to operate electronics in orbit, it is going to get hit. There is a lot of lessons learned from past instances. The good news is, the industry understands how to make the electronics less susceptible to radiation damage. Unfortunately, that makes it a lot more expensive. A total ionizing dose of 25-30 krad is a good parameter for low Earth orbit. But, sometimes we send missions to beyond Jupiter, even outside of the Solar System (bon voyage JHU's *New Horizons*).

Different manufactures of rad-hard components have different approaches, but they can refer to a large body of literature on failure cases. Typically, new electronics is tested for functionality and failure point in Earth-based cyclotrons, usually at University facilities. Failure modes can be summarized as total failure, change in parameters, and wierdness. One common failure mode is latch-up of flip-flops. There can also be transient events, where a device might experience a temporary failure, then return to functionality, a process called annealing.

There are two radiation problem areas: cumulative dose, and single event. Operating above the Van Allen belts of particles trapped in Earth's magnetic flux lines, spacecraft are exposed to the full fury of the Universe.

Earth's magnetic poles do not align with the rotational poles, so the Van Allen belts dip to around 200 kilometers in the South Atlantic, leaving a region called the South Atlantic Anomaly. The magnetic field lines are good at deflecting charged particles, but mostly useless against electromagnetic radiation and uncharged particles such as neutrons. One trip across the Van Allen belts can ruin a spacecraft's electronics. Some spacecraft turn off sensitive electronics every ninety minutes – every pass through the low dipping belts in the South Atlantic.

The Earth and other planets are constantly immersed in the solar wind, a flow of hot plasma emitted by the Sun in all directions, a result of the two-million-degree heat of the Sun's outermost layer, the Corona. The solar wind usually reaches Earth with a velocity around 400 km/s, with a density around 5 ions/cm^3. During magnetic storms on the Sun, flows can be several times faster, and stronger. The Sun tends to have an eleven year cycle of maxima. A solar flare is a large explosion in the Sun's atmosphere that can release as much as 6×10^{25} joules in one event, equal to about one sixth of the Sun's total energy output every second. Solar flares are frequently coincident with sun spots. Solar flares, being releases of large amounts of energy, can trigger Coronal Mass Ejections, and accelerate lighter particles to near the speed of light.

The size of the Van Allen Belts shrink and expand in response to the Solar Wind. The wind is made up of particles, electrons up to 10 Million electron volts

(MeV), and protons up to 100 Mev – all ionizing doses. One charged particle can knock thousands of electrons loose from the semiconductor lattice, causing noise, spikes, and current surges. Since memory elements are capacitors, they can be damaged or discharged, essentially changing state.

Not just current electronics are vulnerable. The Great Auroral Exhibition of 1859 interacted with the then-extant telegraph lines acting as antennae, such that batteries were not needed for the telegraph apparatus to operate for hours at a time. Some telegraph systems were set on fire. The whole show is referred to as the Carrington Event, after British Amateur astronomer Richard Carrington.

Around other planets, the closer we get to the Sun, the bigger the impact of solar generated particles, and the less predictable they are. Auroras have been observed on Venus, in spite of the planet not having an observed magnetic field. The impact of the solar particles becomes less of a problem with the outer planets. Auroras have been observed on Mars, and the magnetic filed of Jupiter, Saturn, and some of the moons cause their "Van Allen belts" to trap large numbers of energetic particles, which cause more problems for spacecraft in transit. Both Jupiter and Saturn have magnetic fields greater than Earth's. Not all planets have a magnetic field, such as Mars, so not all have charged particle belts.

Cumulative dose and single events

The more radiation that the equipment gets, in low doses for a long time, or in high doses for a shorter time, the greater the probability of damage.

These events are caused by high energy particles, usually protons, that disrupt and damage the semiconductor lattice. The effects can be upsets (bit changes) or latch-ups (bit stuck). The damage can "heal" itself, but its often permanent. Most of the problems are caused by energetic solar protons, although galactic cosmic rays are also an issue. Solar activity varies, but is now monitored by sentinel spacecraft, and periods of intensive solar radiation and particle flux can be predicted. Although the Sun is only 8 light minutes away from Earth, the energetic particles travel much slower than light, and we have several days warning. During periods of intense solar activity, Coronal Mass Ejection (CME) events can send massive streams of charged particles outward. These hit the Earth's magnetic field and create a bow wave. The Aurora Borealis or Northern Lights are one manifestation of incoming charged particles hitting the upper reaches of the ionosphere.

Cosmic rays, particles and electromagnetic radiation, are omni-directional, and come from extra-solar sources. Most of them, 85%, are protons with gamma rays and x-rays thrown in the mix. Energy levels range to 10^6 to 10^8 electron volts (eV). These are mostly filtered out by Earth's atmosphere. There is no such mechanism on the Moon, where they reach and interact with the surface.

Solar flux energy's range to several Billion (10^9) electron volts (Gev).

The effects of radiation on silicon circuits can be mitigated by redundancy, the use of specifically radiation hardened parts, Error Detection and Correction (EDAC) circuitry, and scrubbing techniques. Hardened chips are produced on special insulating substrates such as sapphire and diamond. Bipolar technology chips can withstand radiation better than CMOS technology chips, at the cost of greatly increased power consumption. Shielding techniques are also applied. Even a small thickness of aluminum blocks many of the energetic particles. However, a problem occurs when a particle collides with the aluminum atoms, creating a cascade of lower energy particles that can also cause damage. In error detection and correction techniques, special encoding of the stored information provides a protection against flipped bits, at the cost of additional bits to store. Redundancy can also be applied at the device or box level, with the popular Triple Modular Redundancy (TMR) technique triplicating everything, and assuming the probability of a double failure is less than that of a single failure. Watchdog timers are used to reset systems unless they are themselves reset by the software. Of course, the watchdog timer circuitry is also susceptible to failure.

Spacecraft computer systems followed the trend from purpose-built custom units to those based on standard microprocessors. However, the space environment is very unforgiving in many areas, the chief one being radiation. Commercial electronic parts do not last very long in orbit.

So, we have seen control systems for spacecraft go from hardwired logic to a general purpose CPU architecture programmed with software. ASIC's, or Application Specific Integrated Circuits, are also produced in radiation hard versions. This is sort of a throw-back to the hardwired approach, but has its advantages. The next step is systems built from inherently rad-hard FPGA's.

Rad-Hard Software

This is a concept that implements routines that check and self-check, report, and attempt to re-mediate. It is an outgrowth of the testing and self-testing of a computers' functionality, with focus on detection of radiation induced damage. We know, for example, that one of the tell-tales for radiation damage is increasing current draw. At the same time, we monitor other activities and parameters in the system. This partially addresses the problem of operating with non-radiation hardened hardware in a high radiation environment. The baseline ARM-based RaspberryPi has been radiation tested to 150kRad, and was operational at that point.

From formal testing results, and key engineering tools, we define likely failure modes, and possible remediation's. Besides self-test, we will have cross-checking of systems. Not everything can be tested by the software, without some additional hardware. First, we use engineering analysis that will help us define the possible hardware and software failure cases, and then define actions and remediation. This is a software FMEA, failure modes and effects analysis. None of this is new, and the approach is to collect together best practices in the software testing area, develop a library of RHS routines, and get operational experience. Another advantage of the software approach is that we can change it after launch, as more is learned, and conditions change.

Rad Hard software runs in the background on the flight computer, and checks for the signs of pending failure from any known cause. The biggest indicator for radiation damage is an increase in current draw. The mothership cpu cluster monitors and trends current draw across the swarm, and take critical action such as a reboot if it deems necessary. The Rad Hard software will keep tabs on memory by conducting continuous CRC (cyclic redundancy checks). One approach to mitigating damage to semiconductor memory is "scrubbing," where we read and write back each memory locations (being careful not to interfere with ongoing operations). This will be done by a background task that is the lowest priority in the system. Watchdog timers are also useful in getting out of a situation such as a Priority Inversion, or just a radiation-induced bit flip. There will be a pre-defined safe mode for the computer as well. Key state data from just before the fault will be stored. Unused portions of memory can be filled with bit patterns that can be monitored for changes. We must be certain that all of the unused interrupt vectors point to a safe area in the code, in the case of an addressing fault, so this will be reloaded periodically.

Functions within the RHS include current monitoring as a tell-tale of radiation damage, self-diagnosis suite, spurious interrupt test, memory test(s), checksums over code, data corruption testing, memory scrub, I/O functionality test, peripherals test, stack overflow monitoring, and a watchdog timer. A complete failure modes and effects analysis will be conducted over the flight computer and associated sensors and mechanisms, and this will be used to scope the RHS. The systems will keep and report trending data on the flight electronics. In most cases, the only remediation is a reboot.

We can also choose to implement a small, rad-hard recovery computer, using FRAM, which is fairly immune to radiation. The recovery computer receives heart-beat signals from the main computer and take recovery efforts if they are interrupted.

Watchdog Core

For implementations in an FPGA, a separate watchdog unit can be provided in hardware. This will have the same radiation tolerance as the main computer but will be less complex, thus have a smaller cross-section for charged particles. This section can use the TMR approach, rather than the entire chip. This approach was implemented by SiFive in the FE301 and FE540, their fourth generation flash-based FPGA chip. They are immune to radiation-induced changes to configuration.

The FPGA fabric has 150,000 logic cells, which can

implement math blocks, micro (64x18) and large (1024x18) SRAM, They support dual 667 mbps DDR ports.

These parts have a flight heritage. They are manufactured in a 65 nm process. They are qualified to a MIL-STD-883, Class B spec. They support JTAG, as well as 16 Spacewire ports., and PCI Express.

The advantage of having a inherently rad-hard device that can be instantiated with the VHDL for a MIPS architecture, is that you now have a rad-hard MIPS.

MIPS Architecture in Space Flight Applications

This section discusses the application of the MIPS architecture in space flight applications. This has involved the use of the MIPS architecture, instantiated in inherently radiation hard architecture. A MIPS architecture flight computer is currently operating quite successfully outside the bounds of our solar system.

Mongoose

The Mongoose-V is a 32-bit MIPS-architecture microprocessor for space applications It was a radiation-hardened 10–15 MHz version of the MIPS 3000 architecture. The Mongoose was developed by Synova, Inc., with support from the NASA's Goddard Space Flight Center. Harris was the designer, and they used the LSI R3000 design, in a gate array. It was fab-ed in 1 um HCMOS. It was rated at 7.5 MIPS, and included floating point support. The cpu has a 5-stage pipeline. It was fabricated in Silicon-on-Insulator technology, using a rad-hard gate array. Custom peripherals were included, including a dual uart, and EDAC memory. The unit operated on 5 volts.

The Mongoose V processor was a space-rated derivative of the LR-3000 processor of MIPS heritage. It included a 4-kbyte instruction cache and a 2-kbyte data cache, as well as floating-point capability. However, the omission of the memory management unit forced the use of a flat memory model and precluded use of one of the more powerful features of advanced operating systems. It did include a boot prom, dual UART's,and a timer. There was a EDAC unit for the memory. Thirty-two general purpose registers were included

Features of the Mongoose included the MIPS R3000 Instruction Set, the R3010 Floating-point Unit, On-Chip 2KB Data Cache and 4KB Instruction Cache, and speed grades of 10MHz and 15MHz. On-chip Peripherals included Error Detection & Correction, dual Memory Protection, timers, a Dual UART, Expansion Interrupts, a waitstate Generator, and a DRAM Controller. SRAM is supported as well. Either big-endian or little endian operation is possible. The cache can only be flushed if the code doing so is running in non-cached memory. Otherwise, the code will wind up in an endless loop. This is sometimes experienced in the Mongoose V remote debugger. Some users have had problems with the uart, in that it seems to require (or assumes) 2 stop bits.

Radiation Hardness was specified to be LET > 80 MeV-cm2 / mg, and the unit is Latch-up immune. It was built with a silicon-on-insulator technology. It is packaged in a 256-pin ceramic quad flatpack. Prototype units, in quantity 5-9, cost $20,700. Space Flight quality units are around $42,000. These have a LET of greater than 80 MeV-cm2/mg, and the units are latch-up immune. Flight units were available by 1998.

Other spacecraft that use the Mongoose-V include:

NASA's Microwave Anisotropy Probe (MAP), launched in June 2001, carried a Mongoose-V flight computer similar to that on EO-1. The spacecraft measures differences in the temperature of the Big Bang's remnant radiant heat, called the Cosmic Microwave background radiation across the full sky

NASA's X-ray Timing Explorer (XTE) mission used the Mongose as the instrument telemetry controller.

NASA's Microwave Anisotropy Probe (MAP), launched in June 2001, carried a Mongoose-V flight computer similar to that on EO-1. The spacecraft measures differences in the temperature of the Big Bang's remnant radiant heat, called the Cosmic Microwave background radiation across the full sky.

NASA's Space Technology 5 series of microsatellites, air- launched in 2006 from a Pegasus vehicle.

NASA's IceSat Mission, launched into polar orbit in January 2003.

TIMED, or Thermosphere Ionosphere Mesosphere Energetic and Dynamics mission, was launched to study the dynamic of the Mesosphere and Lower Thermosphere portions of the Earth's atmosphere. The Mongoose served as the Control and Data Handling (C&DH) computer. It was launched in December 2001.

EO-1, the Earth Observing Mission, used a Mongoose. The mission launched in 2000, and is currently in extended mission mode.

New Horizons Pluto Mission uses four 12 MHz Mongoose processors. There are two in its Command & Data Handling subsystem, and two more used for guidance and control. . The spacecraft was launched in 2006, and is past Pluto It went past Jupiter in 2007, and Saturn in 2008. It arrived at Pluto in 2015, and is continuing into the Kuiper Belt. Probably due to excessive radiation in the vicinity of Jupiter's magnetotail, on March 19, 2007, the Command and Data Handling computer experienced an uncorrectable memory error and rebooted itself, causing the spacecraft to go into safe mode. The computer fully recovered within two days.

Now in Extended mission mode, New Horizons went on to view   Kuiper belt objects. It conducted one flyby as the year 2019 began. This took it outside the defined boundaries of our solar system to object 2014 MU. Data downlink back to Earth is expected to take 20 months. It continues heading along, and more fly-by images of

Kuiper belt objects are expected. The MIPS-based flight computer is working like a champ. It has been noted that the basic architecture of the Mongoose was used in the earlier Sony Playstation-1. The Playstation did operate at 33 Mhz. But, we're not playing games her, we are studying Kuiper Belt objects.

RH32

The RH-32 was a radiation-hard 32-bit processor chipset developed by the USAF Rome Laboratories for the Ballistic Missile Defense Agency, and produced by Honeywell (later, TRW) for Aerospace applications. It achieves a throughput of 20 MIPS. It was a three-chip set, consisting of Central Processing Unit, Floating Point Unit, and Cache Memory.

The Honeywell and TRW RH32 were developed from a MIPS R3000 model, under sponsorship of the USAF Phillips Lab at Kirkland Air Force Base in New Mexico. It features 16 kilobytes of data cache and 16 kilobytes of instruction cache. It includes four serial I/O channels, four timers, a built-in MIL-STD-1553 bus, 40 programmable I/O lines, and DMA capability. At a module level, the Sun M-bus is supported. The module is available in 100 K rad to one mega-rad hardness with no single-event latch-up. It incorporates IEEE-754 floating-point capability, and memory management features. The RH32 processor is an integral part of the Advanced Spaceborne Computer Module (ASCM). The RH32 is supported by the VxWorks operating system and the gnu-c compiler.

RHC-3000

The RHC-3000 was based on a LSI Logic implementation of the MIPS-3000 cpu, implemented in rad-hard technology by Harris Corporation. It was hard to 1 megaRad, and had a low single event upset error rate. It ran a 20 MHz clock, and a floating point coprocessor. As a microcontroller, it had dual dma channels, dual counter/timers, a 50 Mbps serial I/O bus, and implemented error detection and correction on the main memory and cache.

IDTR-3051

A MIPS architecture IDT R-3051-based embedded controller was used on the Clementine Mission, also called the "Deep Space Program Science Experiment." Launched on January 25, 1994, the objective of the mission was to test sensors and spacecraft components under extended exposure to the space environment and to make scientific observations of the Moon and the near-Earth asteroid 1620 Geographos. The Geographos observations could not be done due to a malfunction in the spacecraft.

The RHC-3000 was based on a LSI Logic implementation of the MIPS-3000 cpu, implemented in rad-hard technology by Harris Corporation. It was hard to 1 megaRad, and had a low single event upset error rate. It ran a 20 MHz clock. It could use a floating point coprocessor. As a microcontroller, it had dual dma channels, dual counter/timers, a 50 Mbps serial I/O bus, and implemented error detection and correction on the main memory and cache.

TX49

The TX49 chip was introduced in 2001 as a 64-bit, radiation tolerant device. This was accomplished by the Hi-Reliability Components Corporation (HIREC) of Japan, under contract to the Japanese Space Development Agency. Toshiba developed the processor core IP in a 64 bit architecture. The host large scale gate array was developed by NEC. Kyoce developed the packaging.

Besides the MIPS instruction set, the chip had a 64-bit data bus, and a 36 bit physical address bus, implementing 64-bit virtual addresses. There were 8k instruction and data caches with error detection and correction. The operating frequency was 25 MHz. The chip implemented floating point. It operated from 3.3 volts, in a temperature range of -40 to +85 degrees C. The packaging was a 302-pin ceramic flat pack.

The approach involved taking the RISC architecture, and implementing it in a inherently rad-tolerant FPGA. That's the game changer.

One of the missions for the TX-49 was the Japanese Engineering Test Satellite-VII, or Kiku-8. It was launched in December of 2006 onboard an Ariane vehicle. It operated until January of 2017. It proved its worth during the earthquake and resulting Tsunami of 2011, providing images in real time.

KOMDIV-32

This was a R-3000 compatible chip, manufactured by the Scientific Research Institute of System Development of the Russian Academy of Sciences. It had an integrated R3010 floating point unit. At least 14 models were produced, from before 2005 to 2016. There was a 64-bit MIPS version, the KOMDIV-64 (2008-2016), dual-issue, superscalar. A much later version was produced in silicon-on-insulator technology in a 675 pin chip, and had RapidIO, ethernet, and pci.

RISC-V implementations in rad-tolerant FPGA's

This section discusses an implementation of the RISC-V architecture in a rad-hard chip. The specific part discussed is the MicroSemi MiV RV32 Risc-V core, It is a soft cpu, based on the 32-bit RISC-V architecture. The manufacturers part number is MiV RV32I MAF_L1_AHB. The chip has 150,000 logic elements, including 462 multipliers, and is built in a 65 uM process.

Microsemi RTG-4

The hardware used to host the RISC-V is a MicroSemi FPGA. We can compare and contrast a MicroSemi soft-core RISC-V in one of these rad-hard FPGA's, with the Mongoose, which is a 32-bit MIPS processor built in a similar process.

A soft-core processor is the architecture description of the chip, that can be implemented in various hardware using logic synthesis.

The hardware can be an FPGA, ASIC, or most any generic configurable hardware platform. (I am trying not to think about a large number of nand gates that I am soldering up, using a print-out.) You can implement multiple soft cores into one "host" giving you a multi-processor, or custom I/O. You can implement memory, but large amounts take a lot of logic space. Essentially, if you can "glue" the modules together with standard interfaces, you can put whatever you want on the hardware, subject to its limitations on logic blocks and I/O. This has been the common approach with the RISC-V architecture. One name for this approach is system-on-a-chip.

Some examples include the Leon, a SPARC architecture, and OpenRISC and OpenSparc.

You can get a hardware description of the architecture to put on your computer. In the case of RISC-V and other open source products, this is free to download. Then you need the toolkit to program you chosen device. This can be available in an open source version, depending on the target hardware. Then you need a "programmer" a way to transfer the logic description into the selected FPGA.

The architecture of the RISC-V is free. Most of the software tools are open source as well. You will need to buy the chip, and a programmer box that hooks up to your computer. You're good to go. (Anyone else remember burning code in a prom? That definitely came after vacuum tubes.)

If you want to make a RISC-V to fly in space on your satellite, it will need to be radiation hardened, or at least radiation tolerant. But, the architectural description of the cpu is radiation-agnostic. You choose a rad-hard/rad-tol FPGA, program it, and you have a rad-hard/rad-tol RISC-V space computer.

The RTG4 device includes JTAG, clocks, controllers for DDR memory, and PCIexpress support. In the FPGA fabric, there are 18x18 math blocks, 64 x 18 microSRAM, and 1024x18 large SRAM. Standard GPIO is included.

The part is available as an engineering sample, MIL-STD-883 military qualification, and in various levels of space flight qualification. The fabric is built in 65 nm technology. It has logic modules, SRAM, and mathblocks. The logic modules have a 4-input LUT's, SRAM, and mathblocks. SEU-hard flip-flops are available. The SRAM is dual port, and can hold 24, 576 bits. A triple-port (2 read, 1 write) SRAM is also available, and can store 1,536 bits. The 374 kbits of non-volatile memory is flash, immune to upsets, and with a TID greater than 100k rad.

The Mathblocks are 18x18 bit signed multiply-accumulate units. They also have addition and subtraction capability.

The MiV_RV32 soft core

The soft core is a description of the logic blocks and their interconnects, in a standardized hardware description language such as VHDL. Besides the RISC-V cpu, it is possible to include additional elements such as timers, a real-time clock, general purpose I/O, watchdog timers, as well as specialized I/O interfaces, including Spacewire.

Really, its that easy. The only catch is, the rad-hard FPGA will cost you a lot more than a desktop model. We'll look at one instance of this process, compared-and contrasted with a "legacy" MIPS space-flight computer, built in rad-hard logic.

The MicroSemi RTG4 is immune to radiation-induced upsets. This is critical, as in an FPGA, radiation damage can change the architecture, if the configuration memory gets hit.

At the design level, it is easy enough to add additional I/O for the CPU core. These would be on the same SoC, and connected to the CPU core internal to the chip. We might want watchdog timers, a real time clock, specialized I/O interfaces such as SPI, I2C, CAN, spacewire, even 1553. These interfaces are discussed briefly later in the book.

Whether we can put them in the same SOC as the RISC-

V depends on the amount of spare logic blocks we have, whether there are spare pins on the chip, and how good the synthesis toolset is.

Microsemi's Development kit for the RT4G-150 part, has 152,824 logic elements, 1 gigabyte of DDR3 memory and 3 gigabytes of SPI flash. It can be purchased with a chip, and additional chips are available. The board supports JTAG and PCI/PCIe interfaces. These are brought out to external connectors. The board also includes 10-gigabit ethernet, spi, and UART support with access to external interfaces. The SPI interface can support external memory.

The board is supported by the Libero SoC software, which can be web-based, for software design and debug. The Libero software is not open source, and a license must be purchased to use it.

Mongoose vs. RISC-V

This section presents a side-by-side comparison of the MIPS-based Mongoose board, and a RISC-V architecture, implemented in a rad-hard FPGA.

	Mongoose	RISC-V
Architecture	MIPS R3000 in single chips asic.	MIPS-3000 (MicroSemi) MiV_RV32 soft core) in RTG-4 FPGA
Flight heritage	6 missions	none to date
Architecture	32 bit	32 bit
Floating point	supported	no
Implementation	silicon-on-insulator	rad-hard FPGA
Data cache	2k	8k
Instruction cache	4k	8k
pipeline	5-stage	5-stage
endian	either	either
SRAM	no	5 megabits
JTAG	no	yes
Clock	10, 15 MHz	300 MHz
EDAC	yes	optional
MMU	no	yes
Memory Protection	yes	yes
Timers	yes	optional **
GPIO	no	optional
Dual UART	yes	optional
PWM	no	optional
QSPI	no	optional
SPI	no	optional
Expansion Interrupts	yes	optional
Waitstate Generator	yes	optional
DRAM Controller	yes	optional
RadHard-LET	>80 *	>100 *
Latch-up immune	yes	yes

Function at TID of	tbd	125 krad
Chip – pins	256	352
Prototype board	$20,700.	$18,000
Flight board	$42,225.	.tbd

* units of MeV-cm^2 / mg
** optional in the listing means these function can be added.

Mongoose specs from:

https://web.archive.org/web/20051226235606/http://www.synova.com/proc/mg5.html

RISC-V specs from: MiV_RV32IMAF_L1_AHB V2.0, MicroSemi.

RTG-4 specs from PB005 Product Brief RTG4 FPGAs, Microsemi

Open Source Software for Space

This section discuss the software, both application code and operating systems, for the RISC-V.

cFE/cFS

The Core Flight Executive, from the Flight Software Branch, Code 582, at NASA/GSFC, is an open source operating system framework. The executive is a set of mission independent re-usable software services and an operating environment. Within this architecture, various mission-specific applications can be hosted. The cFE focuses on the commonality of flight software. The Core Flight System (cFS) supplies libraries and applications. Much flight software legacy went into the concept of the cFE. It has gotten traction within the Goddard community, and is in use on many flight projects, simulators, and test beds (FlatSats) at multiple NASA centers.

The cFE presents a layered architecture, starting with the bootstrap process, and including a real time operating system. At this level, a board support package is needed for the particular hardware in use. Many of these have been developed. At the OS abstraction level, a Platform support package is included. The cFE core comes next, with cFE libraries and specific mission libraries. Ap's are the 5th, or upper layer. The cFE strives to provide a platform and project independent run time environment.

The boot process involves software to get things going after power-on, and is contained in non-volatile memory. cFE has boot loaders for the RAD750 (from BAE), the Coldfire, and the Leon3 architecture. The real time operating systems can be any of a number of different open source or proprietary products, VxWorks and RTEMS for example. This layer provides interrupt handling, a scheduler, a file system, and interprocess communication.

The Platform Support Package is an abstraction layer that allows the cFE to run a particular RTOS on a particular hardware platform. There is a PSP for desktop pc's for the cFE. The cFE Core includes a set of re-usable, mission independent services. It presents a standardized application Program Interface (API) to the programmer. A software bus architecture is provided for messaging between applications.

The Event services at the core level provides an interface to send asynchronous messages, telemetry. The cFE also provides time services.

Aps include a Health and Safety Ap with a watchdog. A housekeeping AP for messages with the ground, data storage and file manager aps, a memory checker, a stored command processor, a scheduler, a checksummer, and a memory manager. Aps can be developed and added to the library with ease.

A recent NASA/GSFC Cubesat project uses a FPGA-based system on a chip architecture with Linux and the cFE. cFE and its associated cFS are available as an architecture for Cubesats in general.

The cFE has been released into the World-Wide Open Source community, and has found many applications outside of NASA.

NASA's software Architecture Review Board reviewed the cFE in 2011. They found it a well thought-out product that definitely met a NASA need. It was also seen to have the potential of becoming a dominant flight software architectural framework. The technology was seen to be mature.

The cFS is the core flight software, a series of aps for generally useful tasks onboard the spacecraft. The cFS is a platform and project independent reusable software framework and set of reusable applications. This framework is used as the basis for the flight software for satellite data systems and instruments, but can be used on other embedded systems in general. More information on the cFS can be found at http://cFS.gsfc.nasa.gov

The compatibility of the cFE and cFS with RISC-V is currently being evaluated.

OSAL

The OS Abstraction Layer (OSAL) project is a small software library that isolates the embedded software from the real time operating system. The OSAL provides an Application Program Interface (API) to an abstract real time operating system. This provides a way to develop one set of embedded application code that is independent of the operating system being used. It is a form of middleware.

cFS aps

cFS aps are core Flight System (cFS) applications that are plug-in's to the Core Flight Executive (cFE) component. Some of these are discussed below.

CCSDS File Delivery (CF)

The CF application is used for transmitting and receiving files. To transfer files using CFDP, the CF application must communicate with a CFDP compliant peer. CF sends and receives file information and file-data in Protocol Data Units (PDUs) that are compliant with the CFDP standard protocol defined in the CCSDS 727.0-B-4 Blue Book. The PDUs are transferred to and from the

CF application via CCSDS packets on the cFE's software bus middleware.

Limit check (LC)

The LC application monitors telemetry data points in a cFS system and compares the values against predefined threshold limits. When a threshold condition is encountered, an event message is issued and a Relative Time Sequence (RTS) command script may be initiated to respond/react to the threshold violation.

Checksum (CS)

The CS application is used for for ensuring the integrity of onboard memory. CS calculates Cyclic Redundancy Checks (CRCs) on the different memory regions and compares the CRC values with a baseline value calculated at system start up. CS has the ability to ensure the integrity of cFE applications, cFE tables, the cFE core, the onboard operating system (OS), onboard EEPROM, as well as, any memory regions ("Memory") specified by the users.

Stored Command (SC)

The SC application allows a system to be autonomously commanded 24 hours a day using sequences of commands that are loaded to SC. Each command has a time tag associated with it, permitting the command to be released for distribution at predetermined times. SC supports both Absolute Time tagged command Sequences (ATSs) as well as multiple Relative Time tagged command Sequences (RTSs).

Scheduler (SCH)

The SCH application provides a method of generating software bus messages at pre-determined timing intervals. This allows the system to operate in a Time Division Multiplexed (TDM) fashion with deterministic behavior. The TDM major frame is defined by the Major Time Synchronization Signal used by the cFE TIME Services (typically 1 Hz). The Minor Frame timing (number of slots executed within each Major Frame) is also configurable.

File Manager (FM)

The FM application provides onboard file system management services by processing ground commands for copying, moving, and renaming files, decompressing files, creating directories, deleting files and directories, providing file and directory informational telemetry messages, and providing open file and directory listings. The FM requires use of the cFS application library

Data Storage (DS

The DS application is used for storing software bus messages in files. These files are generally stored on a storage device such as a solid state recorder but they could be stored on any file system. Another cFS application such as CFDP (CF) must be used in order to transfer the files created by DS from their onboard storage location to where they will be viewed and processed. DS requires use of the cFS application library.

Memory Manager (MM)

The MM application is used for the loading and dumping system memory. MM provides an operator interface to the memory manipulation functions contained in the PSP (Platform Support Package) and OSAL (Operating System Abstraction Layer) components of the cFS. MM provides the ability to load and dump memory via command parameters, as well as, from files. Supports symbolic addressing. MM requires use of the cFS application library.

Housekeeping (HK)

The HK application is used for building and sending combined telemetry messages (from individual system applications) to the software bus for routing. Combining messages is performed in order to minimize downlink telemetry bandwidth. Combined messages are also useful for organizing certain types of data packets together. HK provides the capability to generate multiple combined packets so that data can be sent at different rates.

Memory Dwell (MD)

The MD application monitors memory addresses accessed by the CPU. This task is used for both debugging and monitoring unanticipated telemetry that had not been previously defined in the system prior to deployment. The MD application requires use of the cFS application library .

Software Bus Network (SBN)

The SBN application extends the cFE Software Bus (SB) publish/subscribe messaging service across partitions, processes, processors, and networks. The SBN is prototype code and requires a patch to the cFE Software Bus code. This is now included in the software library.

Health and Safety (HS)

The HS application provides functionality for Application Monitoring, Event Monitoring, Hardware Watchdog Servicing, Execution Counter Reporting (optional), and CPU Aliveness Indication (via UART).

Being open source, you can write your own cFS aps for specific applications, or modify existing ones. However, you should submit them back to the owner (NASA-GSFC) for review and validation so they become a part of the official package.

Operating Systems Supported

The RISC-V architecture can host the open source Fedora linux, Debian, Gentoo, FreeBSD, NetBSD, BuildRoot (embedded). OpenWRT (embedded), Parabola GNU/Linux-libre, OpenSuse, and probably more, as this goes to print.

The following real-time operating systems are supported: RTEMS, Embedded Linux, and FreeRTOS, among others.

Boot process

A brief mention of the boot process is in order, as this small piece of code is responsible for getting the cpu up and working from a reset, or power-on. It is underestimated, and not well understood. Ok, let's discuss what happens when you hit the red button.

In a particular chip architecture, it is hard-wired that upon the occurrence of the reset signal, the instruction pointer gets loaded with a fixed address, and instruction execution starts from that "magic" address." This differs by processor type.

The function of the bootloader, usually stored in non-volatile memory, is to properly configure the hardware, load code from external memory, and jump to that code (which I usually an operating system kernel). One example is GNU GRUB. The bootloader can support the booting of selectable, different operating systems, and perhaps a safe mode. One function that is usually done at boot is a quick POST – power-on self test for the hardware.

A bootloader can operate in separate stages, the first one getting the cpu up and running, and the second one perhaps checking the status of the hardware, then loading the operating system.

Typically, embedded systems, and specifically space computers, must boot into an operational mode quickly, as the spacecraft (or surface lander) might not be in a safe mode.

A different, simpler process is used to return the processor from a "sleep" mode.

The specific boot code for a MIPS processor is "Boot-MIPS." This has various options, depending on what hardware and systems surround the CPU. There is a common "initialize-all units" piece of code, followed by initialize-core-resources," and "initialize system resources." To complicate matters, multicore units may have different boot sequences for each core. A MIPS cpu knows it has to do multiple cores, by reading the CP0 processor ID register. The cpu0 is the first to be booted.

(I will not mention the process for booting a DEC PDP-8 minicomputer, which is burned into my brain, and involved entering a series of octal numbers via switches, and loading a paper tape....)

Afterword

Having an open source alternative for high end embedded computing is a game changer. What will we see as a result of this? Some of the World's most capable supercomputers are MIPS-based. With instantiation in FPGA's, we can easily construct multi-core units on a single chip, and those cores do not need to be identical. We can have as many integer, floating point, and gpu units that will fit. In addition, the interconnection of these units is by internal (to the FPGA) high speed parallel interfaces.

Welcome the new player, MIPS, to the world of IoT and space. Whether it is a long term player, or just another glittery cpu is yet to be seen. As RISC-V gains momentum, the market and the users will decide.

References

Computer Architecture

Bell, C. Gordon and Newell, Allen, *Computer Structures: Readings and Examples*, McGraw-Hill Inc., January 1, 1971, ISBN- 0070043574.

Blaauw, Gerrit A. and Brooks, Frederick P. Jr. *Computer Architecture, Concepts and Evolution,* 2 volumes, 1997, Addison-Wesley, IBN 0-201-10557-8.

Bruess, R. J. *RISC - The Mips-R3000 Family: Architecture, System Components, Compilers, Tools, Applications,* John Wiley & Sons Inc.,1991, ISBN 3800941031.

Burks, Arthur; W. Goldstein, Herman H.; Von Neumann, John *Preliminary Discussion of the Logical Design of an Electronic Computing Instrument*, 1947, MIT Press, originally published in Papers of John Von Neumann on Computing and Computer Theory, ASIN - B0007FXYNS.

Celio, Christopher; Dabbelt, Palmer; Patterson, David A.; Asanović, Krste, "The Renewed Case for the Reduced Instruction Set Computer: Avoiding ISA Bloat with Macro-Op Fusion for RISC-V," (Technical report). University of California, Berkeley,2016, arXiv:1607.02318. UCB/EECS-2016-130.

Chow, Paul *The MIPS-X RISC Microprocessor,* 1989, Springer; ISBN 0792390458.

Comer, Douglas E. *Essentials of Computer Architecture,* Prentice Hall; US Ed edition, 2004, ISBN 0131491792.

Dandamudi, Sivarama P. *Guide to RISC Processors: for Programmers and Engineers,* Springer, 2010, ISBN 144191935X, ASIN: B001E3P3T0.

Godse, A. P. *Microcontrollers & RISC Architecture,* Technical Publications; 1st. edition, 2011, ISBN-9350380390.

Goodman, James; Miller, Karen A *Programmer's View of Computer Architecture: With Assembly Language Examples from the MIPS RISC Architecture,* Oxford University Press, Preliminary ed., 1993, ISBN 0030972191.

Hennessy, John L. and Patterson, David A. *Computer Architecture, Fifth Edition: A Quantitative Approach,* Morgan Kaufmann; (September 30, 2011) ISBN 012383872X.

Reid, T. R. *The Chip: How Two Americans Invented the Microchip and Launched a Revolution,* Random House Trade Paperbacks; Revised edition (October 9, 2001) ISBN 0375758283

Severance, Charles; Dowd, Kevin *High Performance Computing (RISC Architectures, Optimization & Benchmarks)* O'Reilly Media; 2nd ed, 1998, ISBN 156592312X.

Slater, Michael *A Guide to RISC Microprocessors*, Academic Press; 2nd ed. July 1992, ISBN-0126491402.

Slater, Michael *Understanding RISC Microprocessors*: 151 Articles Originally Published in Microprocessor Report Between March 1988 and April 1993, MICROPROCESSORS REPORT, Ziff Davis Press, 1993, ISBN 1562761595.

Sweetman, Dominic *See MIPS Run, 2nd ed, Morgan Kaufmann,* ISBN-0-12-088421-6.

Stakem, Patrick H. *A Practitioner's Guide to RISC Microprocessor Architecture*, 1st Edition, Wiley, 1996, ISBN – 0471130184.

Stakem, Patrick H. *RISC Microprocessors, History and Overview*, 2018, ISBN-1726803600.

MIPS

Bruess, R. J. *RISC - The Mips-R3000 Family: Architecture, System Components, Compilers, Tools, Applications* , John Wiley & Sons Inc.,1991, ISBN 3800941031.

Cmelik, Robert F.; Ditzel, David R.; Kelly, Edmund J.;

"An Analysis of SPARC and MIPS Instruction Set Utilization on the SPEC Benchmarks", Sigplan notices, APR 01 1991 v 26 n 4 Page: 290.

Farquhar, Erin; Philip Bunce. *MIPS Programmer's Handbook*. Morgan Kaufmann Publishers, ISBN-55860-297-6.

Kane, Gerry *MIPS RISC Architecture*, Prentice Hall, 1988, ISBN 0-13-584293-X.

Lincoln, Dan; Smith, Brian "Mongoose: Creation of a Rad-Hard MIPS R3000," 1993, NASA Technical Reports Server, Document ID19940016617.

Harboe-Sorensen, R.,Sund, A. T. "Radiation pre-screening of R3000/R3000A microprocessors," 1992, IEEE Radiation Effects Data Workshop, avail: https://www.researchgate.net/publication/3539157_Radiation_pre-screening_of_R3000R3000A_microprocessors

Hudson, et al "A 10 mips 32 bit RISC Processor with 128 Mbytes/sec Bandwidth", MIPS Computer Systems.

Kaschmitter, J.L. Et al "Operation of commercial R3000 processors in the Low Earth Orbit (LEO) space environment," IEEE Transactions on Nuclear Science,38(6):1415 – 1420, January 1992.

Rowen, Johnson, and Ries, "The MIPS R3010 Floating Point Coprocessor", IEEE Micro, June 1988.

Sweetman, Dominic   *See MIPS Run*, Morgan Kaufmann; 2nd ed, 2006, ISBN 0120884216.

Vail, D. "Estimating the On-Orbit Single Event Upset Behavior of a MIPS R3000 Microprocessor, "Feb 1991, Harris Corporation.

Weiss, Ray; "Third-generation RISC processors", EDN, MAR 30 1992 v 37 n 7 Page: 96.

RISC-V

Acle, Julio Perez, et al "Implementing a safe embedded computing system in SRAM-based FPGAs using IP cores: A case study based on the Altera NIOS-II soft processor," 2011 IEEE Second Latin American Symposium on Circuits and Systems (LASCAS), Bogata, Columbia, Feb. 2011, IEEE Xplore 15 April 2011.

Asanovic, Krste,   *"RISC-V: An Open Standard for SoCs,"2015, avail:* https://www.eetimes.com/author.asp? section_id=36&_mc=RSS_EET_EDT&doc_id=1323406 &page_number=2.

Asanovic, Krste, et al *The Rocket Chip Generator,* UC Berkeley,   avail: https://www2.eecs.berkeley.edu/Pubs/TechRpts/2016/EE CS-2016-17.pdf

Blokdyk, Gerardus *RISC-V a Clear and Concise Reference,* 2018, ISBN-0655348662.

Dos Reis, Anthony *RISC-V Assembly Language*, 2019, ISBN-978-1088462003.

Goodman, James; Miller, Karen *A Programmer's View of Computer Architecture: With Assembly Language Examples from the MIPS RISC Architecture*, Oxford University Press, Preliminary ed., 1993, ISBN 0030972191.

Ledin, Jim *Modern Computer Architecture and Organization: Learn x86, ARM, and RISC-V architectures and the design of smartphones, PCs, and cloud servers,* 2020, ISBN-978-1838984397.

Lee, Yunsup RISC-V "Rocket Chip" SoC Generator in Chisel, High-Performance Computer Architecture (HPCA), 2015. avail:
http://darksilicon.org/hpca/

Patterson, David A., Hennessy, John L. *Computer Organization and Design, RISC-V Edition: The Hardware Software Interface* (The Morgan Kaufmann Series in Computer Architecture and Design), 1st Edition, 2917, ASIN-B0714LM21Z.

Patterson, David, Waterman, Andrew *The RISC-V Reader: An Open Architecture Atlas,* 2017, ISBN-0999249118.

Straka, Bartholomew F. "Implementing a Microcontroller

Watchdog with a Field Programmable Gate Array (FPGA)", 2013, JSC. Avail: https://ntrs.nasa.gov/archive/nasa/casi.ntrs.nasa.gov/2013 0013486.pdf

Waterman, A., K. Asanovi´c, K. (Eds.), *The RISC-V Instruction Set Manual, Volume I: User-Level ISA,* Version 2.2, May 2017. Avail: https://riscv.org/specifications/

Waterman, Andrew, et al The RISC-V Instruction Set Manual Volume II: Privileged Architecture, Version 1.10, avail: https://riscv.org/specifications/privileged-isa/

Resources

https://riscv.org

https://www.idt.com/

RISCV Software Ecosystem, avail - https://riscv.org/wp-content/uploads/2015/02/riscv-software-toolchain-tutorial-hpca2015.pdf

https://www.mips.com/downloads/mips-simd-architecture/

https://www.mips.com/products/architectures/ase/virtualization/

MIPS Instructions

http://www.mrc.uidaho.edu/mrc/people/jff/digital/MIPSir.html

https://web.cse.ohio-state.edu/~crawfis.3/cse675-02/Slides/MIPS%20Instruction%20Set.pdf

The MIPSOpen initiative - https://www.wavecomp.ai/mipsopen.

MIPS ISA - https://wavecomp.ai/mips

https://www.mips.com/?s=mips-v

https://www.mips.com/products/architectures/mips32-2/

https://www.mips.com/products/architectures/mips64/

https://www.allaboutcircuits.com/industry-articles/risc-v-opening-a-new-era-of-innovation-for-embedded-design/

https://wiki.debian.org/RISC-V

https://www.udemy.com/vsd-soc-design-of-the-picorv32-riscv-micro-processor/   (online course)

https://www.sifive.com/boards/hifive1

Synova, Mongoose-V 32-bit MIPS Microprocessor, Architecture Description, Jan. 30, 1997, avail: https://www.electronicsdatasheets.com/manufacturers/synova-inc/parts/mongoosev

https://web.archive.org/web/20060321213756/http://www.synova.com/proc/MongooseV.pdf

http://pluto.jhuapl.edu/Mission/Spacecraft.php#Systems-and-Components.

The HiFive1 Arduino RISC-V board is available from SparkFun, at $68. as of this writing. See:
https://www.sparkfun.com/products/15148
Modular Unified Space Technology Avionics for Next Generation (Mustang), see
http://www.genesisesi.com/mustang.html

http://pluto.jhuapl.edu/Mission/Spacecraft.php#Systems-and-Components.

Conde, Richard F. et al, "Adaptive Instrument Module – A Reconfigurable Processor for Spacecraft Applications," Available:
https://www.researchgate.net/publication

Conde, Richard F. et al "Command and Data Handling in Your Palm," SSC97-I-6. Available:
https://www.researchgate.net/publication

Waterman, Andrew, RISC-V Software Ecosystem, U.C. Berkeley, (Powerpoint), avail:

https://docplayer.net/6864923-Risc-v-software-ecosystem-andrew-waterman-uc-berkeley-waterman-eecs-berkeley-edu.html

SiFive FE310-G000 Manual v2p3; SiFive FE310-G000 Manual v2p3 avail: https://sifive.cdn.prismic.io

Willenx, "A High Performance Deterministic 79R3000-based Embedded System", 9/89, IDT Applications note.

IDT7RS382 Theory of Operation, IDT.

R3051, Single-Chip RISC for Embedded Designs, IDT.

Vr3000, Advanced, High-Performance RISC Microprocessor, NEC Sept 89.

Vr3000 Series, RISC Microprocessor, Electrical Specifications, NEC.

The RISC-V Instruction Set Manual Volume II: Privileged Architecture Version 1.10, May 2017.Avail: https://riscv.org/specifications/

T. Newsome, Ed., RISC-V External Debug Support 0.11, November 2016. Avail:
https://www.sifive.com/documentation/risc-v/risc-v-external-debug-support-0-11/

First Russian MIPS-Compatible Microprocessor, avail: http://dailyrumors.blogspot.com/2007/12/first-russian-mips-compatible.html

https://www.microsemi.com/product-directory/mi-v-embedded-ecosystem/4406-risc-v-cpus

Microsemi, Mitigation of Radiation Effects in RTG4 Radiation- Tolerant Flash FPGAs WP0191 White Paper. Avail:
https://www.microsemi.com/document-portal/doc_view/135027-wp0191-mitigation-of-radiation-effects-in-rtg4-radiation-tolerant-fpgas-white-paper

https://training.mips.com/cps_mips/PDF/Boot_MIPS_Code.pdf

"System Design Using the MIPS R3000/3010 RISC Chipset", MIPS, IEEE Micro, 1989.

LR3010/LR3010A MIPS Floating-Point Accelerator, User's Manual, LSI Logic

LR3000/LR3000A Mips RISC Microprocessor User's Manual, LSI Logic.

LR33000 Self-Embedding Processor, User's Manual, LSI Logic.

IDT RISC, *New Directions for MIPS RISC*, 1990, IDT.

MIPS M/120 RISComputer Technical Overview, MIPS.

RISC Technology Seminar Workbook, 1989, 1990, IDT.

RISC Data Book, 1991, IDT.

System Programmer's Guide, IDT.

Fosdem – 2021, 2020, 2019.

www.wikipedia.org, various.

Specialized I/O

All of these I/O interfaces have been used on spacecraft.

SPI/Microwire

The *Serial Peripheral Interface* (SPI) bus is a full-duplex synchronous serial communication system. It is a master/slave architecture. It uses four wires for the serial clock, the Master-in/slave-out, the master-out/slave-in, and a slave-select. It is the basis for the *JTAG* (Joint Test Action Group)'s diagnostic interface, and has found application in general I/O device interfacing as well. Microwire is a SPI predecessor, that is half-duplex.

I^2C

The *Inter-Integrated Circuit* (I^2C) bus is designed for short-range communication between chips on a board. It is a 2-wire interface that is multi-master, and bidirectional. There are 7-bit slave addresses, so 128 unique devices can be addressed from the current master. It was developed by Philips Semiconductor in the 1980's. It is widely used in embedded systems.

Ethernet

Ethernet is the circa-1973 standard for local area networking technology, widely used for inter-computer data communication. It is defined in standard IEEE 802.3. It is packet-based, and routable, because the packets contain a destination and source address. It can be used over twisted-pair, coax cable, RF, or optical fiber. It makes use of repeaters, hubs, switches, and bridges to extend the network. The Ethernet design was developed at Xerox-PARC, based on the earlier Alohanet protocols.

USB

The *Universal Serial Bus* has a simple 4-wire configuration, 2 wires for power, and two for data. It was developed in 1995. The latest specification, USB-3, provides for up to 5 gigabits per second communication speed. USB is hub-based. There is always a master hub in the system. USB has become the interface of choice for peripherals such as the keyboard and mouse, printers, external hard drives and flash drives, scanners, digital cameras, cell phones, and many others.

The system is designed to support 127 peripherals, but is practically limited to much less than this. USB also supplies power, up to 0.5 amp per port. In many devices, only the power leads are used, to recharge the batteries in the device from the host.

CAN

The *Controller Area Network* (CAN) dates from 1983, and has its origins in industrial control and automation. It was developed by Robert Bosch GmbH in 1986, has been widely used in the automotive industry. It has a message-based protocol, and is a multi-master broadcast serial bus. The theoretical limit for devices on the bus is over 2,000, but a practical limit is about 100. It is a two-wire, half-duplex arrangement. It operates at a conservative 1 mbps, and has error detection and containment features. It is widely used in embedded systems.

RS-232

RS-232 is an electrical and functional telecomm standard dating from 1962. It has an associated EIA standard for the electrical, interface, and timing, but does not specify a connector. The 25-pin D-connector, and the 9-pin D are widely associated with RS-232.

The RS-232 scheme defines a *DTE* (data terminal device) which is a data generator/recipient and a *DCE* (data communication device) which is a channel interface device. This works well for telecomm, where we have a DTE and a DCE at each end, but if a computer is talking to a terminal, which is the DCE? This is handled by having the concept of back-to-back modems, called a *null-modem*, essentially a wire-crossover.

RS-232 runs in a minimum 3-wire scheme for full duplex, but includes a group of control signals to facilitate interface between a device and a modem. The modem translates digital signals into analog signals compatible with the telephone system (i.e., tones in the voice band). RS-232 also has a current loop option.

RS-422/423 synchronous serial

These are ANSI and international standards. They use a balanced voltage, or differential scheme. They can be implemented in a multi-drop or point-point architecture. The standards are for the electrical signaling only. RS-423 uses unbalanced signaling at 4 Mbps, over twisted pair.

These communication schemes use differential drivers over a 2-wire link. Common ground reduces the effect of external noise and cable effects. Voltage swings can be minimized, (faster transmission and less cross-talk) and less susceptible to voltage differences between grounds of transmitter and receiver.

RS-485 is an enhanced RS-422. There can be 32 drivers and 32 receivers on a bi-directional bus. The line typically terminated at the ends by resistors. Addressing uses a polled master/slave protocol.

Spacewire

Spacewire is IEEE standard 1355. It was developed at the European Space Agency (ESA), and represents a full-duplex, point-to-point routable protocol. It operates to 400 megabits per second. Spacewire has found application in the aerospace industry, and space-rated radiation tolerant parts are available, as are IP cores.

MIL-STD-1553

MIL-STD-1553 is a digital time division multiplexed command/response multiplex avionics bus, used in aircraft and spacecraft, and dating from 1973. It uses a coax cable medium, and Manchester bi-phase encoding for code and data transmission. There is a bus controller (BC) and remote terminals (RT's). RT-RT data transmission is allowed, under control for the Bus Controller master. 1553 uses 16-bit words, at a rate of 1 megabit per second. A follow-on standard, 1773, extends the data transmission rate using optical fiber media.

Glossary of Terms and Acronyms

ACM – Association for Computing Machinery; professional organization.

Adas – advanced driver assistant programs, for cars.

AVE - Advanced Vector Extensions.

AI – artificial intelligence.

ALU – arithmetic logic unit.

ANSI – American National Standards Institute.

AON – always on.

API – application program interface; specification for software modules to communicate.

APL – the Applied Physics Laboratory of the Johns Hopkins University.

ARM – microcontroller design from ARM holdings.

ASIC – application specific integrated circuit, custom or semicustom,.

Assembly language – low level programming language specific to a particular ISA.

Async – asynchronous; using different clocks.

AVX - Advanced Vector Extensions.

BAT – branch address translation (cache)

Baud – symbol rate; may or may not be the same as bit rate.

BBL – Berkeley Boot Loader – supports emulation for

soft instructions.

BHT – branch history table.

Big-endian – data format with the most significant bit or byte at the lowest address, or transmitted first.

Binary – using base 2 arithmetic for number representation.

BIST – built-in self test.

Bit – smallest unit of digital information; two states.

Blackbox – functional device with inputs and outputs, but no detail on the internal workings.

Boolean – a data type with two values; an operation on these data types; named after George Boole, mid-19th century inventor of Boolean algebra.

BOOM – Berkeley Out-of-order Machine.

Bootstrap – a startup or reset process that proceeds without external intervention.

BSD – Berkeley Software Distribution.

BTB – branch target buffer.

Buffer – a temporary holding location for data.

Bus – data channel, communication pathway for data transfer.

Byte – ordered collection of 8 bits; values from 0-255

C – programming language from Bell Labs, circa 1972.

Cache – faster and smaller intermediate memory between the processor and main memory.

Cache coherency – process to keep the contents of multiple caches consistent,

C&DH – Command & Data Handling Unit.

cFE – core flight executive, NASA/GSFC flight software.

cFS – Core Flight System, NASA/GSFC.

Chip – integrated circuit component.

CISC – comples instruction set computer.

Clock – periodic timing signal to control and synchronize operations.

CMOS – complementary metal oxide semiconductor; a technology using both positive and negative semiconductors to achieve low power operation.

Compilation – software process to translate source code to assembly or machine code (or error codes).

Coprocessor – another processor to supplement the operations of the main processor. Used for floating point, video, etc. Usually relies on the main processor for instruction fetch; and control.

Cots – commercial, off-the-shelf.

CPLD – complex programmable logic device, not as complex as an FPGA.

CPU – central processing unit.

CQFP – ceramic quad flatpack (chip housing).

CQFP – ceramic quad flat pack.

CRC – cyclic redundancy code, an error control mechanism.

Dataflow – computer architecture where a changing value forces recalculation of dependent values.

D-cache – data cache

DDR – dual data rate (memory).

DDR3 - 3rd version of DDR.

Deadbeef – a known bit pattern, in hex,0xDEADBEEF.

Deadlock – a situation in which two or more competing actions are each waiting for the other to finish, and thus neither ever does.

Device driver – specific software to interface a peripheral to the operating system.

Digital – using discrete values for representation of states or numbers.

Dirty bit – used to signal that the contents of a cache have changed.

DMA - direct memory access (to/from memory, for I/O devices).

Double word – two words; if word = 8 bits, double word = 16 bits.

Dram – dynamic random access memory.

DSP – digital signal processing.

Dual issue – send two instructions out to two execution units similtaneously.

EDAC – error detection and correction.

Epitaxial – in semiconductors, has a crystalline overlayer with a well-defined orientation.

ETU – Engineering Test Unit.

EVA enhanced virtual addressing.

ExaByte – 2^{64} bytes.

Exception – interrupt due to internal events, such as overflow.

Fetch/execute cycle – basic operating cycle of computer; fetch the instruction, execute the instruction.

FIFO – first in, first out. A stack data structure.

Fixed point – computer numeric format with a fixed number of digits or bits, and a fixed radix point. Integers.

Flag – a binary indicator.

Floating point – computer numeric format for real numbers; has significant digits and an exponent.

FLOPS – floating point operations per second.

FMC – FPGA Mezzanine connector.

FOSDEM – Free and Open Source Software Developers European Meeting

FPGA – field programmable gate array.

FPU – floating point unit, an ALU for floating point numbers.

FRAM – ferromagnetic random access memory.

FSBL – first stage boot loader.

Full duplex – communication in both directions simultaneously.

Gate – a circuit to implement a logic function; can have multiple inputs, but a single output.

GCC – Gnu compiler collection.

GEO – geosynchronous or geostationary orbit, 22236 miles for Earth.

Giga - 10^9 or 2^{30}

GNU – recursive acronym for Gnu (is) not Unix.

GPIO – general purpose I/O.

GPU – graphics processing unit. ALU for graphics data.

GRUB – GNU's grand unified bootloader.

GSFC – Goddard Space Flight Center, NASA.

HART – hardware thread.

H1 – MIPS-V model "the Beast."

H2 – MIPS-V model, "Captain"

HAL – hardware abstraction layer.

Harvard architecture – memory storage scheme with separate instructions and data.

HCMOS – high density CMOS.

Hexadecimal – base 16 number representation.

Hexadecimal point – radix point that separates integer from fractional values of hexadecimal numbers.

HDL – hardware description language.

HTIF – host target interface.

I-cache – instruction cache

IDE – Integrated development environment for software.

IDPU – Instrument data processing unit.

IDT – Integrated Device Technology, Inc.

IEEE – Institute of Electrical and Electronic Engineers. Professional organization and standards body.

IEEE-754 – standard for floating point representation and operations.

IEM – intelligent energy monitor.

IMU – inertial measurement unit

Interrupt – an asynchronous event to signal a need for attention (example: the phone rings).

Interrupt vector – entry in a table pointing to an interrupt service routine; indexed by interrupt number.

I/O – Input-output from the computer to external devices, or a user interface.

IOT – Internet of Things.

IP – intellectual property; also internet protocol.

ISA – instruction set architecture, the software description of the computer.

ISO – International Standards Organization.

ISR – interrupt service routine, a subroutine that handles a particular interrupt event.

JTAG – Joint Test Action Group; industry group that lead to IEEE 1149.1, Standard Test Access Port and Boundary-Scan Architecture.

Junction – in semiconductors, the boundary interface of the n-type and p-type material.

Kernel – main portion of the operating system. Interface between the applications and the hardware.

KIKU – Japan's Engineering Test Satellite 8.

Kilo – a prefix for 10^3 or 2^{10}

Kuiper Belt – beyond the orbit of Neptune, 30-astronomical units, a donute shaped area of icy objects.

L1 cache – closest to the cpu.

LE – logic element of an FPGA.

LEO – low Earth orbit.

LET – linear energy transfer. Units of Mev-centimeters squared divided by path length.

LIM – loosely integrated memory; not tightly integrated to a core.

Little-endian – data format with the least significant bit or byte at the highest address, or transmitted last.

Logic operation – generally, negate, AND, OR, XOR, and their inverses.

Loop-unrolling – optimization of a loop for speed at the cost of space.

LRU – least recently used; an algorithm for item replacement in a cache.

LSB – least significant bit or byte.

LSI – chip design company in San Jose; now part of Avago Tech.

LUT – look up table.

Mac – multiply-and-accumulate, operation for digital signal processing,

Macrocell – prefabricated array of logic functions. ALU's, for example.

MADD - multiply-add, a DSP primitive.

Mantissa – significant digits (as opposed to the exponent) of a floating point value.

Master-slave – control process with one element in charge. Master status may be exchanged among elements.

Mathblock - 18x18 bit signed multiply-accumulate units.

Math operation – generally, add, subtract, multiply, divide.

MCU – memory control unit.

MDMX – MIPS Digital Media Extension.

Mega - 10^6 or 2^{20}

MESI – modified, exclusive, shared, invalid, states of a cache coherency protocol.

Microcontroller – microprocessor with included memory

and/or I/O.

Microkernel – operating system which is not monolithic. So functions execute in user space.

Microprocessor – a monolithic cpu on a chip.

Microprogramming – modifying the microcode.

MIL-STD-883 – standard for testing microelectronic devises.

MIMD – multiple instruction, multiple data

MIPS – millions of instructions per second; sometimes used as a measure of throughput; microprocessor without interlcoked pipeline stages.

MIPS32 -32-bit implementation of MIPS architecture.

MIPS64 – 64-bit implementation of MIPS architecture.

MIPS-3D – a SIMD floating point feature for MIPS.

MIPS Open – open source MIPS ISA.

MMS – (NASA) Magnetospheric Multiscale Mission.

MMU – memory management unit; translates virtual to physical addresses.

MMX – SIMD instruction set extension.

MOFF – mostly off.

Mongoose – 32-bit space flight computer, based onMIPS.

MPU – memory protection unit – like an MMU, but without address translation. Also, microprocessor unit, or MIDI   processing unit.

MSB – most significant bit or byte.

MSIO – memory stick I/O.

MSUB – multiply and subtract.

MT – multi-threading.

Multicore – multiple processing cores on one substrate or chip; need not be identical.

Multiplex – combining signals on a communication channel by sampling.

Multithreading – executing multi-threads of execution similtaneously.

Mustang – Modular United Space Technology Avionics for Next Generation.

Mutex – a data structure and methodology for mutual exclusion.

NAN – not-a-number; invalid bit pattern.

NASA – (U.S.) National Aeronautics and Space Administration.

NASDA – National Space Development Agency of Japan.

nm – nanometer.

NMI – non-maskable interrupt; cannot be ignored by the software.

NOR – negated (or inverse) OR function

Normalized number – in the proper format for floating

point representation.

NUMA – non-uniform memory access for multiprocessors; local and global memory access protocol.

NVM – non-volatile memory.

Off-the-shelf – commercially available; not custom.

Opcode – part of a machine language instruction that specifies the operation to be performed.

Open source – methodology for hardware or software development with free distribution and access.

Operating system – software that controls the allocation of resources in a computer.

OTP – one time programmable.

Overflow - the result of an arithmetic operation exceeds the capacity of the destination.

Paging – memory management technique using fixed size memory blocks.

Paired-Single – floating point format with two 32-bit floating point numbers in a 64-bit data structure.

Paradigm – a pattern or model.

Paradigm shift – a change from one way of thinking to another. Can be disruptive or evolutionary.

Parallel – multiple operations or communication proceeding simultaneously.

PCI – peripheral interconnect interface (bus).

Peta - 10^{15} or 2^{50}

Pinout – mapping of signals to I/O pins of a device.

Pipeline – operations in serial, assembly-line fashion.

Pixel – picture element; smallest addressable element on a display or a sensor.

PLIC – platform level interrupt controller.

PMP – physical memory protection.

POST – power on self test.

RTG4 – radiation tolerant FPGA from MicroSemi

PWM – pulse width modulation, for motor control.

QP – quad precision, 128 bit word.

QSPI – Queued serial peripheral interface.

Quad word – four words. If a word = 16 bits, a quad word is 64 bits.

Queue – first in, first out data buffer structure; hardware of software.

Rad-hard – immune to radiation effects, expensive

Rad-tolerant – immune to radiation up to a certain limit.

Radix point – separates integer and fractional parts of a real number.

RAM – random access memory; any item can be access in the same time as any other.

RapidIO – high speed, packet-switched interconnect. Wired or wireless.

RAS – Row address strobe, in dram refresh. Return address stack.

Register – temporary storage location for a data item.

Reset – signal and process that returns the hardware to a known, defined state.

RH32 – rad hard 32 bit MIPS architecture, by USAF Rome Labs.

RHBD - Radiation Hardening By Design.

RISC – reduced instruction set computer.

RO - read-only

ROM – read only memory.

RTG-4 – Rad tolerant FPGA from Microsemi.

RTOS – real time operating system.

RW – read-write.

Sandbox – an isolated and controlled environment to run untested or potentially malicious code.

SDK – system development kit.

SDRAM – synchronous dynamic random access memory.

SEC-DED – single error correct, double error detect,

SEE – single event effects.

Semiconductor – material with electrical characteristics between conductors and insulators; basis of technology processor and memory devices.

Semaphore –signaling element among processes.

SERDES – serialization/deserialization.

Serial – bit by bit.

SEU – single event upset.

SGI – Silicon Graphics, a workstation manufacturer.

Shift – move one bit position to the left or right in a word.

SiFive – fabless semiconductor company., focusing on RISC-V

SIMD – single instruction, multiple data.

SMP – symmetric multiprocessing.

SOC – system on a chip.

Software – set of instructions and data to tell a computer what to do.

Snoop – monitor packets in a network, or data in a cache.

SOC – system-on-a-chip.

Spacewire – high speed spacecraft communications network; following IEEE 1355.

SPI – serial peripheral interface.

SRAM – static random access memory.

SSE – streaming SIMD extensions.

Stack – first in, last out data structure. Can be hardware or software.

Stack pointer – a reference pointer to the top of the stack.

State machine – model of sequential processes.

Superscalar – computer with instruction-level parallelism, by replication of resources.

Synchronous – using the same clock to coordinate operations.

System – a collection of interacting elements and relationships with a specific behavior.

Table – data structure. Can be multi-dimensional.

TDR - trace and debug registers.

Tera - 10^{12} or 2^{40}

Test-and-set – coordination mechanism for multiple processes that allows reading to a location and writing it in a non-interruptible manner.

Thread – smallest independent set of instructions managed by a multiprocessing operating system.

TID – total ionizing dose.

TileLink – open source interconnect standard.

TLB – translation lookaside buffer – a cache of addresses.

TMR – triple modular redundancy

TRAP – exception or fault handling mechanism in a computer; an operating system component.

Triplicate – using three copies (of hardware, software, messaging, power supplies, etc.). for redundancy and error control.

Truncate – discard, cut off, make shorter.

TX-49 - rad tolerant implementation of MIPS-32, Toshiba.

UART – universal asynchronous receiver-transmitter.

Underflow – the result of an arithmetic operation is smaller than the smallest representable number.

Unsigned number – a number without a numeric sign.

Vector – single dimensional array of values.

VHDL- very high level description language; a language to describe integrated circuits and asic/ fpga's.

Virtual memory – memory management technique using address translation.

Virtualization – creating a virtual resource from available physical resources.

VLIW – very long instruction word – mechanism for parallelism.

WDT – watchdog timer.

Wiki – the Hawaiian word for "quick." Refers to a collaborative content website.

WMC – watchdog monitor core.

WO – write only.

Word – a collection of bits of any size; does not have to be a power of two.

Write-back – cache organization where the data is not written to main memory until the cache location is needed for re-use.

Write-through – all cache writes also go to memory.

ZSBL – zero-stage boot loader, usually in ROM.

If you enjoyed this book, you might also be interested in some of these.

Stakem, Patrick H. *16-bit Microprocessors, History and Architecture,* 2013 PRRB Publishing, ISBN-1520210922.

Stakem, Patrick H. *4- and 8-bit Microprocessors, Architecture and History,* 2013, PRRB Publishing, ISBN-152021572X,

Stakem, Patrick H. *Apollo's Computers,* 2014, PRRB Publishing, ISBN-1520215800.

Stakem, Patrick H. *The Architecture and Applications of the ARM Microprocessors,* 2013, PRRB Publishing, ISBN-1520215843.

Stakem, Patrick H. *Earth Rovers: for Exploration and Environmental Monitoring,* 2014, PRRB Publishing, ISBN-152021586X.

Stakem, Patrick H. *Embedded Computer Systems, Volume 1, Introduction and Architecture,* 2013, PRRB Publishing, ISBN-1520215959.

Stakem, Patrick H. *The History of Spacecraft Computers from the V-2 to the Space Station,* 2013, PRRB Publishing, ISBN-1520216181.

Stakem, Patrick H. *Floating Point Computation,* 2013,

PRRB Publishing, ISBN-152021619X.

Stakem, Patrick H. *Architecture of Massively Parallel Microprocessor Systems*, 2011, PRRB Publishing, ISBN-1520250061.

Stakem, Patrick H. *Multicore   Computer Architecture,* 2014, PRRB Publishing, ISBN-1520241372.

Stakem, Patrick H. *Personal Robots*, 2014, PRRB Publishing, ISBN-1520216254.

Stakem, Patrick H. *RISC Microprocessors, History and Overview,* 2013, PRRB Publishing, ISBN-1520216289.

Stakem, Patrick H. *Robots and Telerobots in Space Applications*, 2011, PRRB Publishing, ISBN-1520210361.

Stakem, Patrick H. *The Saturn Rocket and the Pegasus Missions, 1965,* 2013, PRRB Publishing, ISBN-1520209916.

Stakem, Patrick H. *Visiting the NASA Centers, and Locations of Historic Rockets & Spacecraft,* 2017, PRRB Publishing, ISBN-1549651205.

Stakem, Patrick H. *Microprocessors in Space*, 2011, PRRB Publishing, ISBN-1520216343.

Stakem, Patrick H. Computer *Virtualization and the*

Cloud, 2013, PRRB Publishing, ISBN-152021636X.

Stakem, Patrick H. *What's the Worst That Could Happen? Bad Assumptions, Ignorance, Failures and Screw-ups in Engineering Projects, 2014,* PRRB Publishing, ISBN-1520207166.

Stakem, Patrick H. *Computer Architecture & Programming of the Intel x86 Family, 2013,* PRRB Publishing, ISBN-1520263724.

Stakem, Patrick H. *The Hardware and Software Architecture of the Transputer,* 2011,PRRB Publishing, ISBN-152020681X.

Stakem, Patrick H. *Mainframes, Computing on Big Iron,* 2015, PRRB Publishing, ISBN- 1520216459.

Stakem, Patrick H. *Spacecraft Control Centers,* 2015, PRRB Publishing, ISBN-1520200617.

Stakem, Patrick H. *Embedded in Space,* 2015, PRRB Publishing, ISBN-1520215916.

Stakem, Patrick H. *A Practitioner's Guide to RISC Microprocessor Architecture,* Wiley-Interscience, 1996, ISBN-0471130184.

Stakem, Patrick H. *Cubesat Engineering,* PRRB Publishing, 2017, ISBN-1520754019.

Stakem, Patrick H. *Cubesat Operations*, PRRB Publishing, 2017, ISBN-152076717X.

Stakem, Patrick H. *Interplanetary Cubesats*, PRRB Publishing, 2017, ISBN-1520766173 .

Stakem, Patrick H. Cubesat Constellations, Clusters, and Swarms, Stakem, PRRB Publishing, 2017, ISBN-1520767544.

Stakem, Patrick H. *Graphics Processing Units, an overview,* 2017, PRRB Publishing, ISBN-1520879695.

Stakem, Patrick H. *Intel Embedded and the Arduino-101, 2017,* PRRB Publishing, ISBN-1520879296.

Stakem, Patrick H. *Orbital Debris, the problem and the mitigation,* 2018, PRRB Publishing, ISBN-*1980466483.*

Stakem, Patrick H. *Manufacturing in Space,* 2018, PRRB Publishing, ISBN-1977076041.

Stakem, Patrick H. *NASA's Ships and Planes,* 2018, PRRB Publishing, ISBN-1977076823.

Stakem, Patrick H. *Space Tourism,* 2018, PRRB Publishing, ISBN-1977073506.

Stakem, Patrick H. *STEM – Data Storage and Communications,* 2018, PRRB Publishing, ISBN-1977073115.

Stakem, Patrick H. *In-Space Robotic Repair and Servicing*, 2018, PRRB Publishing, ISBN-1980478236.

Stakem, Patrick H. *Introducing Weather in the pre-K to 12 Curricula, A Resource Guide for Educators*, 2017, PRRB Publishing, ISBN-1980638241.

Stakem, Patrick H. *Introducing Astronomy in the pre-K to 12 Curricula, A Resource Guide for Educators*, 2017, PRRB Publishing, ISBN-198104065X.

Also available in a Brazilian Portuguese edition, ISBN-1983106127.

Stakem, Patrick H. *Deep Space Gateways, the Moon and Beyond*, 2017, PRRB Publishing, ISBN-1973465701.

Stakem, Patrick H. *Exploration of the Gas Giants, Space Missions to Jupiter, Saturn, Uranus, and Neptune*, PRRB Publishing, 2018, ISBN-9781717814500.

Stakem, Patrick H. *Crewed Spacecraft*, 2017, PRRB Publishing, ISBN-1549992406.

Stakem, Patrick H. *Rocketplanes to Space*, 2017, PRRB Publishing, ISBN-1549992589.

Stakem, Patrick H. *Crewed Space Stations,* 2017, PRRB Publishing, ISBN-1549992228.

Stakem, Patrick H. *Enviro-bots for STEM: Using Robotics in the pre-K to 12 Curricula, A Resource Guide for Educators,* 2017, PRRB Publishing, ISBN-1549656619.

Stakem, Patrick H. *STEM-Sat, Using Cubesats in the pre-K to 12 Curricula, A Resource Guide for Educators*, 2017, ISBN-1549656376.

Stakem, Patrick H. *Lunar Orbital Platform-Gateway*, 2018, PRRB Publishing, ISBN-1980498628.

Stakem, Patrick H. *Embedded GPU's*, 2018, PRRB Publishing, ISBN- 1980476497.

Stakem, Patrick H. *Mobile Cloud Robotics*, 2018, PRRB Publishing, ISBN- 1980488088.

Stakem, Patrick H. *Extreme Environment Embedded Systems,* 2017, PRRB Publishing, ISBN-1520215967.

Stakem, Patrick H. *What's the Worst, Volume-2*, 2018, ISBN-1981005579.

Stakem, Patrick H., *Spaceports*, 2018, ISBN-1981022287.

Stakem, Patrick H., *Space Launch Vehicles*, 2018, ISBN-1983071773.

Stakem, Patrick H. *Mars*, 2018, ISBN-1983116902.

Stakem, Patrick H. *X-86, 40th Anniversary ed*, 2018, ISBN-1983189405.

Stakem, Patrick H. *Lunar Orbital Platform-Gateway*, 2018, PRRB Publishing, ISBN-1980498628.

Stakem, Patrick H. *Space Weather*, 2018, ISBN-1723904023.

Stakem, Patrick H. *STEM-Engineering Process*, 2017, ISBN-1983196517.

Stakem, Patrick H. *Space Telescopes*, 2018, PRRB Publishing, ISBN-1728728568.

Stakem, Patrick H. *Exoplanets*, 2018, PRRB Publishing, ISBN-9781731385055.

Stakem, Patrick H. *Planetary Defense*, 2018, PRRB Publishing, ISBN-9781731001207.

Patrick H. Stakem *Exploration of the Asteroid Belt*, 2018, PRRB Publishing, ISBN-1731049846.

Patrick H. Stakem *Terraforming*, 2018, PRRB Publishing, ISBN-1790308100.

Patrick H. Stakem, *Martian Railroad*, 2019, PRRB Publishing, ISBN-1794488243.

Patrick H. Stakem, *Exoplanets,* 2019, PRRB Publishing, ISBN-1731385056.

Patrick H. Stakem, *Exploiting the Moon,* 2019, PRRB Publishing, ISBN-1091057850.

Patrick H. Stakem, *RISC-V, an Open Source Solution for Space Flight Computers,* 2019, PRRB Publishing, ISBN-1796434388.

Patrick H. Stakem, *Arm in Space*, 2019, PRRB Publishing, ISBN-9781099789137.

Patrick H. Stakem, *Extraterrestrial Life*, 2019, PRRB Publishing, ISBN-978-1072072188.

Patrick H. Stakem, *Space Command*, 2019, PRRB Publishing, ISBN-978-1693005398.

CubeRovers, A Synergy of Technologys, 2020, PRRB Publishing, ISBN-979-8651773138.

Robotic Exploration of the Icy moons of the Gas Giants. 2020, PRRB Publishing, ISBN- 979-8621431006

Hacking Cubesats, 2020, PRRB Publishing, ISBN-979-8623458964.

History & Future of Cubesats, PRRB Publishing, ISBN-979-8649179386.

Hacking Cubesats, Cybersecurity in Space, 2020, PRRB Publishing, ISBN-979-8623458964.

Powerships, Powerbarges, Floating Wind Farms: electricity when and where you need it, 2021, PRRB Publishing, ISBN-979-8716199477.

Hospital Ships, Trains, and Aircraft, 2020, PRRB Publishing, ISBN-979-8642944349.

2020/2021 Releases

CubeRovers, a Synergy of Technologys, 2020, ISBN-979-8651773138

Exploration of Lunar & Martian Lava Tubes by Cube-X, ISBN-979-8621435325.

Robotic Exploration of the Icy moons of the Gas Giants, ISBN- 979-8621431006.

History & Future of Cubesats, ISBN-978-1986536356.

Robotic Exploration of the Icy Moons of the Ice Giants, by Swarms of Cubesats, ISBN-979-8621431006.

Swarm Robotics, ISBN-979-8534505948.

Introduction to Electric Power Systems, ISBN-979-8519208727.

Centros de Control: Operaciones en Satélites del Estándar CubeSat (Spanish Edition), 2021, ISBN-979-8510113068.

Exploration of Venus, 2022, ISBN-979-8484416110.

Patrick H. Stakem, *The Search for Extraterrestial Life,* 2019, PRRB Publishing, ISBN-1072072181.

The Artemis Missions, Return to the Moon, and on to Mars, 2021, ISBN-979-8490532361.

James Webb Space Telescope. A New Era in Astronomy, 2021, ISBN-979-8773857969.